YOUR KNOWLEDGE HAS VALUE

- We will publish your bachelor's and
  master's thesis, essays and papers

- Your own eBook and book -
  sold worldwide in all relevant shops

- Earn money with each sale

Upload your text at www.GRIN.com
and publish for free

Uqbah Iqbal

Japanese Interests to Singapore during Lee Kuan Yew Era

GRIN Publishing

Bibliographic information published by the German National Library:

The German National Library lists this publication in the National Bibliography; detailed bibliographic data are available on the Internet at http://dnb.dnb.de .

This book is copyright material and must not be copied, reproduced, transferred, distributed, leased, licensed or publicly performed or used in any way except as specifically permitted in writing by the publishers, as allowed under the terms and conditions under which it was purchased or as strictly permitted by applicable copyright law. Any unauthorized distribution or use of this text may be a direct infringement of the author s and publisher s rights and those responsible may be liable in law accordingly.

Imprint:

Copyright © 2015 GRIN Verlag, Open Publishing GmbH
Print and binding: Books on Demand GmbH, Norderstedt Germany
ISBN: 978-3-668-01571-5

This book at GRIN:

http://www.grin.com/en/e-book/302852/japanese-interests-to-singapore-during-lee-kuan-yew-era

GRIN - Your knowledge has value

Since its foundation in 1998, GRIN has specialized in publishing academic texts by students, college teachers and other academics as e-book and printed book. The website www.grin.com is an ideal platform for presenting term papers, final papers, scientific essays, dissertations and specialist books.

Visit us on the internet:

http://www.grin.com/

http://www.facebook.com/grincom

http://www.twitter.com/grin_com

Japanese Interests to Singapore during Lee Kuan Yew Era

'Learning from Japan' is a word of wisdom expressed by Lee Kuan Yew to speed up the industrialization process between Singapore and Japan. This motto gives great meaning in an effort to further strengthen Singapore's economy in particular, and the ASEAN economies generally, in helping the region achieve a self-sufficient level expected. By making Japanese an economy example, Singapore will be able to acquire the skills and expertise of Japan in the field of economy, science and technology to serve as a stimulus to progress the region. Japan has cultural characteristics that are closer and suitable example for ASEAN countries because its eastern elements. Singapore's move to emulate Japan is made because the country's ability to develop its economy from collapse after the Second World War to became a respected industrial country.[1]

Leadership characteristics which enable Japan to emerge as the champion of the world economy and full attention to the needs of development and economic development, without neglecting the elements of Asian culture are inspiring Singapore. To explore the successes achieved by Japan, the country's economic strategy needs to be understood first.[2] One simple indicator that can be used to show the importance of the relationship between Singapore and Japan is the visit made by the Prime Minister of Singapore, Lee Kuan Yew to Japan. Between 1969 to 1979, he traveled to Japan nine times and the aim is certainly not to travel, but as he said himself, "Every time I visit Japan, its economic progress and social remind me of what can be achieved if there is a country that has people who are hardworking and talented, educated and well-organized ... ".[3]

On 17 June 1973, the new Singapore ambassador to Japan, Wee Mon Cheng expressed his hope to encourage the Japanese people to invest and divert their modern technology to Singapore. He will also encourage the Japanese people to buy light company goods made in Singapore.[4]

---

[1] Norman Suratman, Mencontohi kemajuan dari negara Matahari Terbit... in *Berita Harian*, 15 September 1983, p. 4.
[2] Ibid.
[3] Zainul Abidin Rasheed, Peranan Jepun yang lebih besar diinginkan utk industri2 tempatan in *Berita Harian*, 18 November 1979, p. 4.
[4] Anonymous, Berharap rakyat Jepun tambah tanaman modal di S'pura in *Berita Harian*, 17 June 1973, p. 14.

In January 1975, Singapore's ambassador to Japan, Cheng Wee Moon described the year 1975 as an important year for Japanese investors to invest in Singapore. The worldwide economic downturn brings new opportunities for the development and restructuring of companies in Singapore. With that the Japanese businessmen and companies should take this opportunity to develop together a strong company for mutual benefits. They should be prepared to feel the benefit when world economic activity and opportunities in the Southeast Asian region live again. The world market scenario has caused many workers in Singapore discharged from factories that use a lot of labor, such as electronics, timber and garments which takes half of Singapore's labor force. Because they are young, they have become a useful source of labor and can be trained by new factories.[5]

In September 1975, Singapore's ambassador to Japan, Wee Moon Cheng state Japanese must refrain from damaging role played by Southeast Asian countries in developing their economic strategy. This is because the healthy economic situation in the region will affect the state of the Japanese economy. Not wrong for Japan to pay more attention to the Middle East and Latin America, but Japan should not forget that Southeast Asia is as important as the United States to Japan. He did not imagine what will happen to the economic development and security of Japan if Japan one day found it was unable to carry out free trade with the countries of Southeast Asia and the loss of one-fifth of the country's total foreign trade income.[6]

Although Singapore is a small country, but it and Japan have a lot of items to be offered in exchange in the fields of trade, industry and investment opportunities. Japan reminded of the importance of South East Asia, trade statistics in 1974 showed that Southeast Asia has accounted for about 20 percent of Japan's outside revenue, similar to what it get from the United States. Japan's trade with the Middle East amounted to only 15 percent of its foreign income and with Latin America only 13 percent. Singapore can offer a lot of convenience to Japanese traders include services, finance, technology, and as a base for the production of goods. But Singapore's economic progress may be increased if Japan encourage more

---

[5] Anonymous, Pengusaha2 Jepun diseru lebih banyak melabur modal di Singapura in *Berita Harian*, 22 January 1975, p. 8.
[6] Anonymous, Jepun digesa giatkan lagi dagangan dengan S'pura. Berbagai2 kemudahan disediakan utk kepentingan bersama – Wee in *Berita Harian*, 12 September 1975, p. 2.

investment firm, providing broader training facilities and introduce and import more products to Singapore.[7]

In November 1975, Singapore's ambassador to Japan, Wee Moon Cheng state people in the ASEAN region amounted to 250 million people is a market for any investments in Singapore. Goods made in Singapore can also be exported to all over the world as it has been described as the world market.[8] On 23 December 1975, he urged Japanese investment members to devote more capital in Singapore in order to benefit both countries. Japan is the largest trading partner to Singapore in 1974. Japan also urged to buy more goods from Singapore especially light industrial products that are cheaper than they produce themselves. As a central market in South East Asia, Singapore would provide more business with Japan. Japan is also the most active foreign investors in Singapore in 1974. Japanese companies will get many benefits by removing their products in Singapore. The establishment of Consulate General office in Osaka is the result of Wee Moon Cheng efforts to promote cultural and economic activities between the two countries.[9]

In February 1978, Singapore's ambassador to Japan, Wee Mon Cheng state the number of Japanese investments in Singapore in that year will continue to grow because Singapore has low prices for land to build factories, Singapore has a lower rate of pay with a good yield and the value of the Yen is higher in Singapore in accordance with the exchange rate.[10] In August 1978, he stated investment from Japan to Singapore at the end of 1978 is expected to increase because Japanese producers feel the cost of higher wages, soaring land prices and foreign exchange rates that are less well established to undertake investment in their countries. Due to this, Singapore businessmen duties are to provide a place and a good supply of labor to Japanese businessmen. Singapore can be Japanese option because of its good location and sufficient facility. Japanese investment in Singapore has increased by 31 percent in 1977 and this is expected to continue. Another advantage achieved by Singapore of the appreciation of the Yen is tourism. This is because the Japanese people find it too expensive to travel from Tokyo to Osaka than holidays from Japan to ASEAN. An increase of 35.8 percent of visitors from Japan to Singapore is a good sign in a tourist company and the situation is believed to

---

[7] Ibid.
[8] Anonymous, 250 juta rakyat ASEAN pasaran yg baik untuk Jepun in *Berita Harian*, 22 November 1975, p. 2.
[9] Anonymous, Peniaga2 Jepun digesa labur lebih banyak di S'pura in *Berita Harian*, 24 December 1975, p. 2.
[10] Anonymous, Beberapa buah syarikat Jepun akan buka cawangan, labur $200j. di Singapura in *Berita Harian*, 16 February 1978, p. 8.

continue for a long period of time.[11] This is because the presence of Japanese tourists in large numbers in Singapore are due to the large number of Japanese investment here and the Japanese forming the largest expatriate group in number. ASEAN tourists also visit Singapore for business, shopping or just a path on the way home or abroad. On 27 February 1980, Deputy Prime Minister of Singapore, Dr. Goh Keng Swee said that Japanese investments have provided employment opportunities for Singaporeans other than improving government sources.[12]

On 27 March 1984, Senior Minister of State (Prime Minister's Office), Lee Khoon Choy state Economic Development Board (EDB) is started negotiations to obtain the cooperation of a number of Japanese multinational companies (MNCs) to sponsor Singaporean study at leading universities in Japan. The main purpose of this effort is to enable those who have been choosen to learning the work attitude and management practiced by Japanese companies. Hopefully they will become the dealer to transfer high technology and Japanese investment knowledge in intensive to Singapore. Japanese investment quality in Singapore has improved from time to time since 1960. Japan has managed to take strategic measures in Singapore in accordance with the Singapore government's call to encourage companies to use a more sophisticated and less labor to establish here. Japanese companies in Singapore have succeeded in producing goods with higher added value. They use equipment to reduce dependence on labor. Apart from that, they also provide training and improve the skills of its employees in the use of companies' machinery and computer technology.[13]

In August 1984, the Minister of Finance which also Minister of Trade and Industry of Singapore, Dr. Tony Tan said that one advantage Singapore have compared to its two closest competitors, South Korea and Taiwan are the ability to move a new company as soon as possible. However, it should pay attention to the cost factor. Singapore will also focus on enterprises that require high skills such as enterprise services that can be spared from trade protection policy.[14]

---

[11] Anonymous, Lebih banyak pelaburan dari Jepun diduga: Dubes in *Berita Harian*, 22 August 1978, p. 8.
[12] Anonymous, Pelaburan Jepun bantu S'pura: Goh in *Berita Harian*, 27 February 1980, p. 1.
[13] Anonymous, Cari penaja rakyat belajar di varsiti Jepun. Biar pelajar kita dalami sikap kerja di sana in *Berita Harian*, 28 March 1984, p. 8.
[14] Anonymous, Tiga faktor boleh jejas pelaburan in *Berita Harian*, 9 August 1984, p. 1.

On 30 May 1986, Minister of State (Trade and Industry and Home Affairs) of Singapore, Dr. Lee Boon Yang expressed the commitment of Japanese investments during 1985 exceeded the level of annual investment over the past five years. He was pleased to see in recent more Japanese companies in Singapore who has switched from production to consumption industrial products, development and design engineering. Singapore government hopes to encourage more Japanese investors expand their activities than simply the production of research, development and design of products as well as establish a comprehensive business centers in Singapore. With the facilities available, Japanese companies are expected to make Singapore as a good center to expand their development activities to cover the needs of countries in the Asia-Pacific region in particular and the world in general. In June 1986, the Finance Minister of Singapore, Dr. Richard Hu said that the presence of Japanese companies in Singapore is small, but the fund management sector showed favorable growth. He was referring to the presence of two Japanese companies that have operations in Southeast Asia and has established investment companies in Singapore to manage their money.[15]

On 12 August 1986, Minister of State (Trade and Industry and Home Affairs of Singapore) of Singapore, Dr. Lee Boon Yang urged Japanese companies to take a more active part in its Local Companies Improvement Plan (LCIP) to help local companies reduce costs and improve production quality. Program conducted by the Small Business Bureau (SEB) is not only to provide assistance in terms of financial and other, but also help their suppliers to increase productivity and improve quality. It will also reduce the price of materials and services suppliers. The cost reduction will benefit both parties because it would make Singapore industrial products can compete in the market.[16]

On 15 July 1988, the Prime Minister of Singapore, Lee Kuan Yew declared Singapore can play an important role in the strategy of Japanese multinational companies to expand its activities in the world. From Singapore, Japanese companies can meet the needs of the market not only in their country but also the region and the world market. They can also make use of the labor force in the ASEAN region which is larger and cheaper. Japan will be a major player in the ASEAN region's economic growth next century. It can strengthen the relationship with other countries in Asia through trade and transfer of technology and

---

[15] Anonymous, Minebea bentuk firma pelaburan bernilai $70 juta in *Berita Harian*, 27 June 1986, p. 2.
[16] Anonymous, Kos dan mutu: Gesaan kepada syarikat Jepun in *Berita Harian*, 13 August 1986, p. 3.

expertise that is independent through investments. Economic relations can also be reinforced through cultural and social exchange and human relations more frequently.[17]

In June 1989, First Deputy Prime Minister, Goh Chok Tong stated that companies from Japan and Singapore could work together to explore opportunities for trade and investment in areas that has many employee and supply of natural resources.[18] On 14 February 1992, the Singapore Malay National Organisation (PKMS) remind Singapore society to stop criticizing Japan for the atrocities and suffering that brought during the Second World War. It is feared could affect the country's investment here, and worse still encourage them to produce war equipment to expand its military power again.[19] On 9 May 1993, the Prime Minister of Singapore, Goh Chok Tong state more Singaporean entrepreneurs should penetrate the Japanese market. Singaporean entrepreneurs should not just look to China.[20]

In January 2000, Singapore's Minister for Trade and Industry, Brigadier-General (Deployment) George Yeo declared Free Trade Agreement (FTA) between Singapore and Japan will further strengthen Japan's commitment in Southeast Asia in the long term. The agreement is also expected to promote free trade in the Asia Pacific region.[21] In May 2005, the Prime Minister of Singapore, Lee Hsien Loong state Singapore's government supports Japan's intention to become a permanent member of the Security Council of the United Nations (UN). This is because the contribution of Japan to the United Nations during this time makes it ideal as a member of the Security Council.[22]

Japan interests to Singapore's economic is reflected in the official and economic trips from Singapore to discuss economic relations between the two countries, exchanged views on the international financial situation and strengthen ties between the people of both countries. Among them is the visit of Prime Minister of Singapore, Lee Kuan Yew on 22 October 1979,[23] a visit of 40 Singapore representatives headed by the Vice President of the Chamber

---

[17] Anonymous, Jadikan Singapura sebagai pusat niaga, seru PM in *Berita Harian*, 16 July 1988, p. 1.
[18] Anonymous, Jepun diajak teroka bersama peluang labor in *Berita Harian*, 15 June 1989, p. 1.
[19] Anonymous, PKMS: Usah lagi kecam Jepun in *Berita Harian*, 15 February 1992, p. 16.
[20] Anonymous, PM gesa usahawan tembusi Jepun in *Berita Harian*, 10 May 1993, p. 1.
[21] Anonymous, FTA bakal kukuh komitmen Jepun in *Berita Harian*, 18 January 2000, p. 6.
[22] Anonymous, Singapura sokong hasrat Jepun di PBB in *Berita Harian*, 19 May 2005, p. 1.
[23] Anonymous, Lee tiba di Jepun in *Berita Harian*, 22 October 1979, p. 1.

of Commerce and Singapore Chinese Industry, Lim Tow Yong on 30 September 1984,[24] a trade mission led by Deputy Minister of Trade and Industry, Brigadier-General (Reserve) Lee Hsien Loong on 11 May 1986,[25] the visit of Prime Minister of Singapore, Lee Kuan Yew in October 1986,[26] an investment mission led by the Chairman of the Economic Development Board (EDB), Philip Yeo on 23 February 1987[27] and the visit of the Minister of Trade and Industrial, Brigadier-General (Deployment) Lee Hsien Loong on 22 November 1987.[28]

In 1978, the Japanese government has received a total of 408 trainees from Singapore and sent a total of 106 Japanese technical experts to Singapore. In the period between 1973 to 1978, the number of Singapore workers trained in Japan is 1,707 persons and the number of Japanese workers that were sent to Singapore is 470 persons. The establishment of the Singapore-Japan Training Centre in Jalan Bukit Merah characterized by Lee Kuan Yew as a symbol of Japan's contribution to Singapore's efforts to obtain higher industrial skills that will enhance Singapore's industrial workers towards middle technology.[29]

On 10 May 1973, the government of Singapore and Japan reached an agreement that the problem of ships navigation safety through the Straits of Malacca and stability of Southeast Asia are the two main things that concern them along.[30] In April 1977, six Japanese companies have formally expressed their interest to invest in the construction of a petro-chemical company in Singapore.[31] On 28 July 1983, the Ministry of International Trade and Industry of Japan (MITI) has decided to increase the Japanese government aid in petrochemical projects in Singapore. The officers stated that MITI is planning investments

---

[24] Anonymous, 5 wakil DPMS sertai konvensyen di Jepun in *Berita Harian*, 27 September 1984, p. 3. See also Anonymous, Hasil lawat ke Jepun dlm pertemuan DPMS in *Berita Harian*, 16 October 1984, p. 3.
[25] Anonymous, Usaha EDB tarik pelaburan Jepun melalui temuan khas in *Berita Harian*, 2 April 1986, p. 8. See also Anonymous, Usaha tarik pelaburan Jepun ke sini in *Berita Harian*, 9 May 1986, p. 1. See also Anonymous, Fujitsu rancang tambah $40j untuk hasilkan IC. Ekoran pelaburan2 baru in *Berita Harian*, 6 June 1986, p. 11. See also Anonymous, Hsien Loong ketuai misi ke Jepun in *Berita Harian*, 8 May 1986, p. 2.
[26] Anonymous, PM Lee selamat pulang ke tanahair in *Berita Harian*, 21 October 1986, p. 1.
[27] Anonymous, Pengerusi EDB ketuai misi labor ke Jepun in *Berita Harian*, 23 February 1987, p. 2.
[28] Anonymous, BG Lee ketuai misi galak labur ke Jepun in *Berita Harian*, 23 November 1987, p. 1.
[29] Zainul Abidin Rasheed, Peranan Jepun yang lebih besar diinginkan utk industri2 tempatan in *Berita Harian*, 18 November 1979, p. 4.
[30] Anonymous, Lee-Tanaka sepakat... in *Berita Harian*, 11 May 1973, p. 1.
[31] Anonymous, Enam tunjuk minat sertai bersama projek petro-kimia Jepun — S'pura in *Berita Harian*, 29 April 1977, p. 6. See also Anonymous, Tawaran dari Sumitomo utk projek petrokimia. DI PULAU AYER MERBAU DGN BELANJA $1.7b in *Berita Harian*, 31 March 1976, p. 8.

totaling 8.4 billion yen (about $ 74.2 million) in addition to the capital of three billion yen ($ 26.5 million).[32]

On 14 May 1986, Japan's biggest economic newspaper, Nihon Keizai Shimbun publishing advertisement about Singapore benefits as an investment center. Singapore is making the advertising campaign in a big way to attract and lure Japanese investors to invest in the country. The published black and white advertisement in a full-page is believed to be worth more than $ 100,000 and funded by the Economic Development Board (EDB). The board has allocated $ 4 million for advertising and it plans to launch a campaign in various international publications. EDB was trying to get at least $ 1.1 billion worth of investments in one of the worst times in business in Singapore. In making this project success, EDB facing competition from other countries, including Ireland, North and South America, Hong Kong and Taiwan that are often advertised in international media. The first advertisement featuring bamboo grove graphic painting highlights the hidden forces of Singapore. Bamboo is a symbol of strength and flexibility. Singapore's strengths is like bamboo grove, lies with the government and its people. Their determination will ensure Singapore remains a business center in Asia.[33]

In March 1987, Singapore's Minister for Trade and Industry, Brigadier-General (Deployment) Lee Hsien Loong state is more meaningful to look at Singapore's trade balance with the rest of the world, rather than trying to achieve a balance of trade with Japan. Part of Singapore's trade deficit with Japan is imported goods from Japan to Singapore, but then re-exported to other countries. Japan not long ago is an important market for Singapore, but the country's investment here increased the number of Singaporean exports to other countries. However, the Singapore government is always looking for ways to increase exports of goods to Japan's local factory.[34]

On 10 May 1993, the government of Singapore and Japan formally agreed to work together to provide technical assistance to developing countries in Asia and Africa, including sending experts to these countries. On 17 March 1995, Singapore and Japan signed an agreement to increase trade and business cooperation between the two parties. The agreement was signed

---

[32] Anonymous, Petrokimia: Ikrar Jepun in *Berita Harian*, 28 July 1983, p. 1. See also Anonymous, Runding rumit minggu ini. Projek kompleks petrokimia in *Berita Harian*, 4 October 1983, p. 1. See also Anonymous, Kompleks petrokimia mula operasi Feb '84 in *Berita Harian*, 20 October 1983, p. 8.
[33] Anonymous, Kempen iklan untuk tarik pelaburan Jepun ke sini in *Berita Harian*, 14 May 1986, p. 1.
[34] Anonymous, Laburan yang dijanji syarikat Jepun in *Berita Harian*, 7 March 1987, p. 2.

by Chairman of the Kansai Economic Federation (Kankeiren), Tetsuro Kawakami with the President of the Singapore Manufacturers Association (SMA), Robert Chua.[35]

Singapore also joined Asean Expo 95 in Osaka, Japan, which starts 21 September until 25 September 1995. Together with five other ASEAN member countries, namely Malaysia, Indonesia, Thailand, Philippines and Brunei, Singapore will display the goods and services in the exhibition by aims to increase bilateral trade between the countries with Japan.[36] In 1995, the investment ratings agency, Moody's Investors Service Inc. listed Singapore banks as the safest and strongest bank in Asia, outpacing Hongkong and Japan banks. Singapore became the third most attractive real estate investment in Southeast Asia after Australia and New Zealand, according to a quarterly review of the international real estate consultancy firm, Knight Frank in 1998.[37]

On 13 January 2002, Singapore and Japan signed a free trade agreement that will pave the way for closer economic cooperation between the two countries. This agreement is known as Economic Partnership for a New Era of Japan-Singapore. On 2 August 2005, the government of Singapore and Japan's largest bank, Mizuho Bank signed an agreement that allows the government to use customer information for the purpose of the bank's financial investments here.[38] Singapore is among the 20 leading countries in the world with attractive economics for foreign direct investment (FDI), according to the Investment Prospects Survey 2007-2009 FDI on 5 October 2007. The Council of the United Nations Organization for Trade and Development (UNCTAD) said Singapore was 16th place in the list.[39]

---

[35] Darwis Said, Peniaga S'pura, Jepun ikat perjanjian tingkat kerjasama in *Berita Harian*, 18 March 1995, p. 16.
[36] Anonymous, Singapura sertai Pameran Asean di Osaka in *Berita Harian*, 21 September 1995, p. 12.
[37] Anonymous, S'pura ketiga paling menarik bagi pelaburan hartanah in *Berita Harian*, 18 July 1998, p. 27.
[38] Anonymous, Singapura dan bank terbesar Jepun meterai janji in *Berita Harian*, 3 August 2005, p. 6.
[39] Anonymous, S'pura antara 20 destinasi pilihan pelaburan langsung in *Berita Harian*, 6 October 2007, p. 23.

Reference

Anonymous. 1973. Lee-Tanaka sepakat.... *Berita Harian*, 11 May: 1.

Anonymous. 1973. Berharap rakyat Jepun tambah tanaman modal di S'pura. *Berita Harian*, 17 June: 14.

Anonymous. 1975. Pengusaha2 Jepun diseru lebih banyak melabur modal di Singapura. *Berita Harian*, 22 January: 8.

Anonymous. 1975. Jepun digesa giatkan lagi dagangan dengan S'pura. Berbagai2 kemudahan disediakan utk kepentingan bersama – Wee. *Berita Harian*, 12 September: 2.

Anonymous. 1975. 250 juta rakyat ASEAN pasaran yg baik untuk Jepun. *Berita Harian*, 22 November: 2.

Anonymous. 1975. Peniaga2 Jepun digesa labur lebih banyak di S'pura. *Berita Harian*, 24 December: 2.

Anonymous. 1976. Tawaran dari Sumitomo utk projek petrokimia. DI PULAU AYER MERBAU DGN BELANJA $1.7b. *Berita Harian*, 31 March: 8.

Anonymous. 1977. Enam tunjuk minat sertai bersama projek petro-kimia Jepun — S'pura. *Berita Harian*, 29 April: 6.

Anonymous. 1978. Beberapa buah syarikat Jepun akan buka cawangan, labur $200j. di Singapura. *Berita Harian*, 16 February: 8.

Anonymous. 1978. Lebih banyak pelaburan dari Jepun diduga: Dubes. *Berita Harian*, 22 August: 8.

Anonymous. 1979. Lee tiba di Jepun. *Berita Harian*, 22 October: 1.

Anonymous. 1980. Pelaburan Jepun bantu S'pura: Goh. *Berita Harian*, 27 February: 1.

Anonymous. 1983. Petrokimia: Ikrar Jepun. *Berita Harian*, 28 July: 1.

Anonymous. 1983. Runding rumit minggu ini. Projek kompleks petrokimia. *Berita Harian*, 4 October: 1.

Anonymous. 1983. Kompleks petrokimia mula operasi Feb '84. *Berita Harian*, 20 October: 8.

Anonymous. 1984. Cari penaja rakyat belajar di varsiti Jepun. Biar pelajar kita dalami sikap kerja di sana. *Berita Harian*, 28 March: 8.

Anonymous. 1984. Tiga faktor boleh jejas pelaburan. *Berita Harian*, 9 August: 1.

Anonymous. 1984. 5 wakil DPMS sertai konvensyen di Jepun. *Berita Harian*, 27 September: 3.

Anonymous. 1984. Hasil lawat ke Jepun dlm pertemuan DPMS. *Berita Harian*, 16 October: 3.

Anonymous. 1986. Usaha EDB tarik pelaburan Jepun melalui temuan khas. *Berita Harian*, 2 April: 8.

Anonymous. 1986. Hsien Loong ketuai misi ke Jepun. *Berita Harian*, 8 May: 2.

Anonymous. 1986. Usaha tarik pelaburan Jepun ke sini. *Berita Harian*, 9 May: 1.

Anonymous. 1986. Kempen iklan untuk tarik pelaburan Jepun ke sini. *Berita Harian*, 14 May: 1.

Anonymous. 1986. Pelaburan Jepun dijangka terus meningkat. *Berita Harian*, 31 May: 32.

Anonymous. 1986. Fujitsu rancang tambah $40j untuk hasilkan IC. Ekoran pelaburan2 baru. *Berita Harian*, 6 June: 11.

Anonymous. 1986. Minebea bentuk firma pelaburan bernilai $70 juta. *Berita Harian*, 27 June: 2.

Anonymous. 1986. Kos dan mutu: Gesaan kepada syarikat Jepun. *Berita Harian*, 13 August: 3.

Anonymous. 1986. PM Lee selamat pulang ke tanahair. *Berita Harian*, 21 October: 1.

Anonymous. 1987. Pengerusi EDB ketuai misi labor ke Jepun. *Berita Harian*, 23 February: 2.

Anonymous. 1987. Laburan yang dijanji syarikat Jepun. *Berita Harian*, 7 March: 2.

Anonymous. 1987. ANGKA BERBICARA. *Berita Harian*, 12 October: 4.

Anonymous. 1987. BG Lee ketuai misi galak labur ke Jepun. *Berita Harian*, 23 November: 1.

Anonymous. 1988. Jadikan Singapura sebagai pusat niaga, seru PM. *Berita Harian*, 16 July: 1.

Anonymous. 1989. Jepun diajak teroka bersama peluang labor. *Berita Harian*, 15 June: 1.

Anonymous. 1992. PKMS: Usah lagi kecam Jepun. *Berita Harian*, 15 February: 16.

Anonymous. 1993. PM gesa usahawan tembusi Jepun. *Berita Harian*, 10 May: 1.

Anonymous. 1993. Kerjasama Jepun-S'pura. *Berita Harian*, 11 May: 1.

Anonymous. 1995. Singapura sertai Pameran Asean di Osaka. *Berita Harian*, 21 September: 12.

Anonymous. 1995. Penilaian: Bank S'pura paling kukuh di Asia. *Berita Harian*, 7 December: 1.

Anonymous. 1998. S'pura ketiga paling menarik bagi pelaburan hartanah. *Berita Harian*, 18 July: 27.

Anonymous. 2000. FTA bakal kukuh komitmen Jepun. *Berita Harian*, 18 January: 6.

Anonymous. 2001. FTA Singapura-Jepun hampir lengkap. *Berita Harian*, 6 September: 8.

Anonymous. 2002. Singapura, Jepun meterai janjian perdagangan bebas. *Berita Harian*, 14 January: 1.

Anonymous. 2005. Singapura sokong hasrat Jepun di PBB. *Berita Harian*, 19 May: 1.

Anonymous. 2005. Singapura dan bank terbesar Jepun meterai janji. *Berita Harian*, 3 August: 6.

Anonymous. 2007. S'pura antara 20 destinasi pilihan pelaburan langsung. *Berita Harian*, 6 October: 23.

Darwis Said. 1995. Peniaga S'pura, Jepun ikat perjanjian tingkat kerjasama. *Berita Harian*, 18 March: 16.

Norman Suratman. 1983. Mencontohi kemajuan dari negara Matahari Terbit…. *Berita Harian*, 15 September: 4.

Zainul Abidin Rasheed. 1979. Peranan Jepun yang lebih besar diinginkan utk industri2 tempatan. *Berita Harian*, 18 November: 4.